LOOKING IN
THE
MIRROR

HEAL YOUR **PAST**
TO HELP YOUR
FUTURE

by

Jayla Anderson Westbrook

Other Contributors:

Anas J.
Book Cover Design
Fiverr (2023)

Robyn S. Brownlow
Editing and Formatting
Robyn Shanae Consultancy, LLC

Dedication

This book is for every little girl, every woman, and every person who has ever shared this reality.
I want to Thank You for being the STRONG person you are.

You are so beautiful, and I am so thankful that I was able to be a vessel for your voice to take the stage and be heard.
Thank you for being so brave to fight daily for your healing.

You are ALL Superheroes...

FORWARD

by Trarina Paige

It is an honor to praise the incredible **Jayla Anderson Westbrook**, a multi-talented young lady who has grown into a confident and inspiring writer.

Watching her journey from a church pew baby to a phenomenal actor, and now a skillful writer, is nothing short of amazing. Being proud of you is an understatement. Jayla's talent and determination are truly inspiring, and her presence in the world is necessary. Her confidence, energy, encouragement, smarts, and unwavering faith in GOD are just a few of the qualities that make her a light in this world.

Jayla's gift for storytelling is truly remarkable. Her writing is captivating, and her words have the power to move and inspire others. When I read this book, I couldn't help but think, *"how is she so dope at this age!?"*

I am elated about all the incredible things that GOD has in store for her. As the scripture says, *"Eyes have not seen, nor ears heard, nor has it entered into the heart of man the things which GOD has prepared for those who love Him..."*

Jayla, with my whole heart, I absolutely love you. And it is an honor to witness this incredible journey. I do not doubt that you will continue to change the world one book at a time, and I cannot wait to see all the amazing things that are in store for you. Go take this world by storm, Jayla.

We are all cheering you on!

Table of Contents

PART 3: THE AWAKENING...

Author's Note

WARNING!
THIS BOOK CONTAINS THE FOLLOWING TOPICS:
*RAPE, SEXUAL ASSAULT, MISCARRIAGE,
ALCOHOLISM, CHILD ABUSE, AND NEGLECT.*
IF YOU ARE TRIGGERED BY, OR CAN NOT HANDLE
READING ABOUT EITHER OF THESE TOPICS,
PLEASE DO NOT READ THIS BOOK.

ALSO, THIS IS NOT AN AUTOBIOGRAPHY.
ALTHOUGH THESE EVENTS CAN AND POTENTIALLY
HAS HAPPENED TO SOMEONE IN REAL LIFE, THIS
STORY IS NOT PERSONALLY RELATED TO ME OR
ANYONE ASSOCIATED WITH ME.

THIS BOOK IS A WORK OF REALISTIC FICTION.
ANY RELATION TO ACTUAL EVENTS, PEOPLE, OR
PLACES IS NOT PURPOSEFUL BUT ENTIRELY
COINCIDENTAL.

AGAIN, THIS IS PURLEY REALISTIC FICTION.
I AM AN ARTIST, AND I'M SENSITIVE ABOUT MY
STUFF... SO BE EASY. AMEN...
THANK YOU AND ENJOY!

LOVE,
JAYLA ANDERSON WESTBROOK
(DUH, I WROTE THE BOOK!)

NEED HELP?

If you or someone you know is struggling with the effects of sexual assault or are currently dealing with sexual assault, please look at this list of resources that can help.

****

National Sexual Assault Hotline: available 24 hours
- 1-800-656-4673
- www.rainn.org

Domestic and dating violence hotline: available 24 hours
- 800-799-7233
- Thehotline.org

National human trafficking hotline: available 24 hours
- 888-373-7888
- Humantraffickinghotline.org

****

YOU ARE NOT ALONE!
YOU CAN DO THIS!
I BELIEVE IN YOU!!!

HELP IS AVAILABLE...

PROLOGUE

When asked, *"How did you write this book?"*, I simply say, *"it's by the grace of GOD"* because it's true. I had no outline, no plot pyramid, and no money. All I had was a computer and a brain.

While writing this, I doubted myself; I felt unworthy of writing a book with such meaning. I gave up about 45 times. What should have taken me 2 days to write took me 2 weeks. I started, stopped, and started again. I didn't feel like it was good enough; I didn't feel like it was long enough. I cried, and I pulled about 12 all-nighters. Even though I had a lot of setbacks, I continued to persevere, and I finally made it!

I decided to write about this topic because I read an article on Gen-Z breaking generational curses. It really spoke to me because, for years, sexual assault has been seen as something that just *"happens"*. However, as I thought about it, I realized it was much deeper than that. This happens because, in earlier generations when traumatic incidents happened to someone, they likely never dealt with it. Instead, they would consequently pass the pain down to their children. From there, the children often either **became** monsters themselves or they became another survivor... OR BOTH! Because of that article, I now know the name of that cycle and how I could use my pen to break it.

I started writing this book at the end of middle school, but when summer came, I got distracted. In November of 2022, I started reading a book called *"Grown" by Tiffany D. Jackson*, and I immediately realized that I had to finish what I started. I grabbed my computer, sat in the back of the library during lunch, and wrote. Words poured through my fingers like water. GOD gave me exactly what to say and how to say it. Every period, comma, italic, space, date, word, and name were on purpose. I wrote it down even if I didn't know how a specific sentence or chapter would connect to the book. I rewrote, deleted, and brought back so many things throughout this book I started to get whiplash.

I took my time with this book because it is a delicate topic, and because I wanted to be as accurate and thorough as possible. I didn't want to say the wrong thing and mess up people's ideas of sexual assault survivors. I wanted to ensure that when people read this book, it would spark a conversation and connect with people. I wanted people to cry and laugh and I wanted to speak to every little girl, boy, woman, or man who has ever had their innocence taken from them. I wanted them to know that they are not alone and that I hear and see them. I wanted them to see someone fictional or not overcome something that they may think is impossible.

I wanted them to know that there are people who care and want the best for them. I wanted them to understand that what happened to them doesn't have to define them. I wanted them to know that they are not tainted, that they are not garbage. I wanted them to see that they are somebody and that their voices deserve to be heard.

One of my inspirations was the story of Tamar in the Bible *(2 Samuel chapter 13)*. One of the reasons why this story was so inspirational was because Tamar didn't get a happy ending. She was never heard from again after what happened to her due to how her society worked. This spoke to me because this happens in our societies now, especially in the black community.

We instill shame into survivors of assault, and we silence them. The idea of being *"too grown"* or *"too fast"* is a prime example. We sexualize natural body developments like breasts and hips. We make them something that black girls should feel ashamed about or make them something that should be hidden.

So when black girls get assaulted, they carry this guilt with them because they automatically assume that because their bodies are shaped more maturely, or because no matter what clothes they wear, people can still see their bodies in the outfit, is why these things happen to them. We make them believe that if they were to speak out, they would break the family up.

We make their voice a Pandora's box, never to be opened, filled with dirty secrets. Secrets full of poison that slowly spreads until it reaches their brain and until they can no longer even recognize themselves. Until they have spent 20 or 30 years just surviving and not living at all. Until every limb, every bone, and vessel is rotten. Until they either die or use drugs or sex, or alcohol as a temporary boric acid to put the poison to sleep until they can handle it.

Instead of protecting our young girls by not having the monsters around, we make them change their clothes when *"Uncle Pookie"* comes over. Or we abuse them for telling the truth to people outside the house because we believe that *"what happens in this house stays in this house"*. What are children supposed to do when the people who are supposed to check under the bed for monsters become the monsters?

Even though we can't excuse the actions or reactions of our family members to what happens to survivors, we also have to take into consideration that these systems are not new. They are constant and have been here for generations, hence the *generational curse*. So it's sometimes not them just being outright malicious towards survivors, but sometimes it's just all they know. That's why I wrote this book to help educate the people in our community and help us to do better and protect the ones after us.

When reading this book, I want you, as the reader, to take in the experiences of Aniyah. I want you to try putting yourself in her shoes and feel her pain, her joy, and her hurt. I want you to pay attention to how she describes her everyday life and feelings. I want you to take a trip into her world. I want you to listen to her. I want you to respond to her. I want you to accept her.

As you read, you will go through so many emotions, and you will have so many opinions. I want you to vocalize them. because there is no way to start a conversation without words. I want you to be okay with being vulnerable with yourself and with the people you choose to have these conversations with. It's okay to cry and not understand. I want you to reread, highlight, and take a break. This book is heavy, so if you need to stop and take a breather, allow yourself to do so. It will always be here when you're ready for it.

So, I guess the question is …. Are You Ready?

Are you ready to start to unpack the things that have been hidden for so long... The things that make you uncomfortable... The things you tried to forget...?

If so, it's time to turn the page...

INTRODUCTION

There was a girl…

A girl with *hope*,

A girl with dreams...

Her dreams where stolen…

Her joy was stolen,

Her ESPWA was stolen…

She tried to stuff her past in the back of her mind,

But instead, it was stuffing her lungs.

So she began to choke and drown…

Will she become forever lost in the sea of her past?

Or will she Finally

Look… In…

The Mirror…

Part 1:

"The Slumber"

Chapter 1:

APRIL 9TH, 2011

"What does it say, Aniyah?" I stand there sweating profusely like a football coach after a winning game when the team dunks water over them. I don't want to look. I can't look. My hands shake as I turn over the test slowly, praying that God changes the lines.

As soon as I turn over the test, my mom grabs it from my hands and looks for herself. My mother's face went blank as if no emotion was left in her body. I just wanted the floor to swallow me whole. I feel the two red lines blaring into my soul like my screen does when I get a question wrong on Kahoot. It's crazy to know that something as simple as two little red lines could ruin my entire life.

The air in my lungs seems to just disappear. My life flashes before my eyes as all my plans and my dreams just disappear. Taken by two little red lines. I could feel the anger radiating from her body onto me like a heat wave in California. It stung and burned. Her stare penetrates my body like a blade.

"How could you do this to me!?" This is what she said as she threw the test across the room at me. It hit me in my chest; even though it was just a long piece of plastic, it hurt.

"You just couldn't keep your grown tail away from him. You just had to take every ounce of happiness from me, right? Are you happy now? Answer me, Aniyah. Are you happy?" My body shakes as she yells. She is so mad that I can see the salvia forming in her mouth as she talks.

"I didn't mean to, momma, I swear. I didn't try to. He came to me, not the other way around. He was too strong. I'm sorry. Please believe me." I say as hot tear streams cover my face.

"So now you lying, huh? You think I would believe you didn't come on to him. Aniyah, please get out of my face now. GET OUT!"

Why won't she believe me…

****

"I hear Brenda's got a baby,
But Brenda's barely got a brain…
A damn shame,
The girl can hardly spell her name…"

- Brenda's Got a Baby
Tupac

****

Chapter 2:

April 9th, 2022

I wake up to the sun burning my face and the smell of must and alcohol. I haven't moved out of this spot, let alone shower. Jack Daniels sits next to me, judging me and taunting me. There are 5 empty bottles of him scattered on my bed.

I stare at my ceiling, trying to convince myself to move. I say everything I can, but it doesn't work… Until my alarm rings for the 9,124th time. I pulled off the covers and forced myself up a little too fast. And before I knew it, Jack was pouring out of my mouth like a muddy river. Yet, somehow, now I feel much better than I did 2 minutes ago.

I hate nothing more than having to look in the *mirror*, so I look at the sink. I turn on the faucet just slightly to see the water drip slowly into the drain. I get lost in it, trying to guess when the next droplet will fall. Hoping that it doesn't double drip. *Drip. Drip. Drip…*

I turn on the shower to the hottest temperature; I like it that way. It's therapeutic, because I feel like just as it burns my skin, the water is burning all those dark and ugly feelings away. I contemplate not going to work and just crawling back into bed and disappearing. However, I need my rent to be paid. So, I throw on clothes, grab my computer, briefcase, and my smile off my dresser and leave.

****

Got a five in my pocket, wanna buy me some gin.
I drop a gas in the tank, let me think it over again.
Cause I'd rather be drunk,
And drive away from here, then to be sober…
So sober Yeah.
No friends coming through, I think I lost them all.
No man to take their place so, I decided to this call.
Whoa… And I'd rather be drunk

- Drunk
Tweet

****

Chapter 3:

APRIL 16ᵀᴴ, 2011

My mom and I sit in the doctor's office.
My legs are shaking. My ears are burning. I'm
hoping and praying that the pregnancy test was
wrong and that I'm NOT pregnant. False positives
happen all the time, right? The doctor enters the
room with a concerned look but tries to play it off
with a quick smile. She looks at me,

"Hi, you must be Aniyah; I am Dr. Stephanie. Your
urine sample came back positive, so you are indeed
pregnant. Is this your mother?" She turns to my
mom, who doesn't look up at her. She acts as if SHE
is the one who should be embarrassed. As if I am
not the one who's 15 and having a whole child! She
pretends as if she couldn't have prevented this. But
she could have. She could have protected me...

"You know, there are options in these situations;
you could decide to keep the fetus or not; it is

completely up to you". I don't want to keep it. How can I care for a baby when I'm still one myself?

"Is it covered by our insurance if she decides not to keep it?" My mom says, still not looking up.

"No, not fully. The co-pay would be $120 if Aniyah wanted to terminate her pregnancy." I thought, wow, $120 is a lot of money to get rid of a baby I didn't want anyway.

"Ok, well, she will be keeping it; ain't nobody got that type of money for her."

"Momma, please!"

"Aniyah, you are keeping it, and that's final! Now let's get out of this doctor's office." I start to cry. The doctor looks even more concerned and unsure how to interject. Why is this happening to me? I can't live like this. I can't. My life is over before it ever really began.

We were quiet the whole ride home. I stared out the window, looked at the sky, and became angry with GOD. How could he let this happen to me?

Why me, out of all people. I used to believe in GOD before *HE* came. I used to believe in heaven, angels, and peace. But now, all I believe in is hell, because I'm already living in it...

****

I wanna believe, but I'm having a hard time seein' pass
What I see right now, I see right now.
I Wanna be free, but when I try to fly,
I realize I don't know how. No one showed me how.
I wish I could see that this mess I'm in
Will really work out for my good; You said it would...
So if you can hear me, can you give me a sign?
Because I don't feel you like I should. Please, if you could.
My faith is almost gone. I can't hold on much longer.
Take this cup from me
But if you choose not to, please
Help me believe; Can I believe?
Let me believe; I wanna believe...
I'm no good on my own, please give me another chance..
It's hard to believe in what I can't see.
To give you my will, cause you're what's better for me.
You can look in my eyes and see I Wanna Believe...

- Help Me Believe
Kirk Franklin

****

Chapter 4:

APRIL 16TH, 2022

I don't talk that much to my colleagues, but I always wonder what its like for them. To go home happy, to come here happy, wake up happy, and go to sleep happy. It's so much happiness, is it ever draining? Tiring? Because feeling like this is tiring.

I can wear all the Gucci and Louis Vuitton I want, but no band aid is strong enough. No towel is good enough to cover or clean or heal the mess that is my life…

    I don't WANT to be dark.

    I don't WANT to be cold.

    I don't WANT to be empty.

It's just hard to find light in this. And if I do, can I trust it? Will it last? Or will it be just as temporary as my band aid… Sometimes I wonder what my life would be like if *HE* never came. If I wouldn't have lost my childhood. If I hadn't lost my *Espwa*.

I can smile for a picture; I can laugh for a moment
but when that moment is over. When that smile
fades. I'm still here in the *upside-down* begging for
someone to hear me screaming and pull me up. Pull
me up from every branch of lies and every branch
of abuse. I hope someone will pull me up from it
all…

****

Thought I found a way, thought I found a way out.

But you never go away, so I guess I gotta stay now.

Oh, I hope some day I'll make it out of here…

Even if it takes all night or a hundred years.

Need a place to hide, but I can't find one near…

Wanna feel alive outside, I can't fight my fear.

Isn't it lovely, all alone?

Heart made of glass my mind of stone

Tear me to pieces, skin to bone.

Hello, welcome home…

- Lovely
Billie Eilish and Khalid
****

Chapter 5:

"I Know She Knew"
(poem)

I know she knew...
There is no way she didn't know.

I know she knew...
When he would leave her bed
in the middle of the night,
to sneak into my room.

Or when he would make her
take my brother to school,
And would tell her that he would take me
because he wanted to "bond" with me.
Even though it was entirely out of his way for work,
and I never showed up at school...

He never showed that much interest in my brother.
JUST ME.
So I know she knew...

The way I would always
beg to go with her to the store
if that meant I didn't have to stay home with him.

I know she knew...
A mother SHOULD know!

Yet, she never said anything.
Never even defended me.
Never stopped him.
Never believed me.
She Blamed ME!

How could she blame me?
What was I to do?

I know she knew...

I know she heard my cries...
And aching pains...

I KNOW SHE KNEW.

Chapter 6:

July 9th, 2011

It's officially been 4 months. I can't keep anything down. My clothes barely fit, and I can't sleep. My future haunts me. I don't leave my room anymore, even though *He* is not here. He left when my mom told *Him* that I was pregnant. *He* wanted nothing to do with it. It's funny how *He* has a choice. When I am stuck reaping the consequences of *His* actions. *His* words still haunt me every single day.

"You are nothing..."

I tell myself I don't believe *Him*…. but I do…. Why else would she choose *Him* over me? If I was worth something, she would have stood up for me. She would have said something. She would have protected me. I am here right now only because, when I hear MY child's heartbeat, it's enough to keep me fighting one more day...

The rhythm is like the baseline in jazz….
It's so strong… It's as though their heart is not just
pumping for them, but for me too. Maybe in that,
there IS *hope*...

****

So many times, I tried to run away...
I couldn't find rest cause there was no hiding place.
Then I heard a voice from deep within say,
This is Who I Am, I no longer can pretend...
And I Was Created for This...
Ooooh, I Was Created for This...
And I, yeah, yeah, yeah, yeah....
And I Was Created for This...

- I Was Created for This
Tweet

****

JULY 9TH, 2022

When I was growing up, there were so many rules. Rules that you had to follow as a black girl. Rules that were supposed to protect you.

Rules like:

1. **NO** red lipstick (*being fast*)
2. **NO** straight hair (*being grown*)
3. **NO** colored hair (*looking wild and crazy*)
4. **NO** lip gloss with any color in it (*and it can't be too glossy*)
5. **DO NOT** sit on a man's lap if you're over 8years old (*being all up in men's face*)
6. **DO NOT** play with your male cousins (*only the female ones*)
7. You **MUST** wear clothes that cover your body when uncles come over, so you don't provoke them. (*or you must stay in your room*)
8. **NO** hoop earrings (*trying to be fast*)
9. **NO** shorts (*too revealing*)
10. **NO** long hair (*trying to be cute*)
11. **NO** make-up (*trying to be grown*)
12. **NO** red nail polish (*looking like a night walker*)
13. **NO** tight or short cut dresses (*you're advertising*)

Just to name a few...

These rules were supposed to protect you from the spirits that laid beneath the people who you would least expect. The dangers of the minds of men. The threat of the insecurities in women and their need for men. The dangers of what happens when the lights go off. The damage that doesn't get spoken of once they happen. The dangers of hands that wander too far.

I followed these rules…

I believed in these rules…

So why did I STILL get hurt?

What made ME different?

I hate the way I look. I feel nasty and tainted, as if I were milk that had spoiled beyond the 3-day expiration point. I feel worthless. No one would want a girl that was too fast or grown. So, I don't date. I don't go out. I put all that energy into work.

I work 6 days a week, sometimes 17 hours a day. I overbook myself; I overprove myself, so they won't realize how tainted I am and throw me away, just like she did… Will they throw me away?

The good thing about most garbage is a lot of it can be recycled. However, some pieces can never be turned new, and some parts can never be cleaned. cleaned. *Mirrors* that can never be fixed once broken. Plastic that will forever drift into the abyss. Precious flowers, that can never be uncrushed...

Chapter 8:

SEPTEMBER 13TH, 2011

We are 6 months in now, and my mom still
is not speaking to me. My brother tries to talk to
me, but my mom won't let him. I throw myself into
school to distract myself. Before my situation, I had
always wanted to be a lawyer. Now, my only focus
is doing enough to at least get my diploma. Most
people hate going to school, but I love it. It helps
me escape the suffocating vines of my upside-down
life. I've just learned to ignore the stares and the
whispers. And even the rumors.

People hate what they don't understand. Honestly, I
don't even understand what's happening half the
time. The baby kicked for the first time yesterday,
and it scared the mess out of me. It was a wake-up
call because I need to find a way to make money to
take care of this baby. I asked my guidance
counselor for a work permit form and for a list of

jobs I can apply for. I pray that one says Yes! She also told me about WIC, which is like the baby version of an EBT card.

I applied for 5 jobs in two weeks. I did 3 job interviews, but 2 never called back. The movie theater was the only one that did. It was my only option, so I took it. I'm about to be a mom. It's not about me anymore. I know that now...

****

I don't really have any archenemies,
My only villain is myself...
I'm not quite exactly who I wanna be, hmm...
I can't be anybody else, and I can't do it all.
So, call me superwoman,
But I know I'm not that strong... Nooo
Because I cry more than a little,
And if I'm superwoman, I'm flying in the rain.
And I wonder, will it ever get old,
Being a superwoman smiling through the pain...

- Superwoman
Meghan Trainor

****

Chapter 9:

September 13th, 2022

I ran out of alcohol...

And I can't find my car keys...

So I am freaking out...

When I'm at work, I don't need it because I'm surrounded by people. But when I get home, I'm by myself, and I must face myself, and I can't do that... So I drink.

When I drink, I don't remember. I don't know how I was able to pass law school with the number of whiskey bottles I was going through. I'm what you call a *functioning alcoholic*. But if you ever call me that, I will deny it and call you crazy.

But Deep...

Deep...

Deep Down...

I know it's true. Hey, it is what it is! At this point, anything to ease the pain will do. I walk into Benny's ashamed with my head down. This is my

3rd trip this week. I grab my usuals, and I come here so much that I know exactly how much it will cost, so I just carry exactly how much I need.

I walk up to the cashier, and she stares at me for about 5 seconds before ringing up my items. I know what she's thinking without her having to say anything. She rings them slowly as if she is giving me a chance to change my mind. I don't change my mind though. I need to get rid of these feelings. I need them gone.

Before she can even tell me the total, I just hand her the money and grab my bag, and almost run out of the store. I open one of the bottles before even leaving the parking lot, and I drink, and I drink, and I drink. I drink until I have to come up for air. When I breathe, I feel my feelings pulling to the back of my brain.

MY FIX, MY FIX, MY FIX...

****

I tried to drink it away...

I tried to put one in the air.

I tried to dance it away...

I tried to change it with my hair.

I ran my credit card bill up...

Thought a new dress make it better.

I tried to work it away...

But that just made me even sadder.

Well, it's like Cranes in the Sky,

Sometimes I don't want to feel those medal clouds...

- Cranes in the Sky
Solange

****

Chapter 10:

OCTOBER 21ST, 2011

There is a saying, "*A mother always knows*".
And I knew... It had been 3 days, and the baby
didn't kick once. I thought maybe it was just
sleeping a lot, but then the 7th day rolled around,
and I got nervous. I asked my mom if this was
normal or if she could take me to the doctor.
She refused. But I knew something was wrong.

It was 9 A.M., my stomach cramped as if it was
flipping inside out. And then I started bleeding...
I can't be bleeding. You don't bleed when you are
pregnant. Something MUST be wrong. It must be!
A mother Always knows...

"Momma, I think something's wrong with the baby.
My stomach hurts really bad, and I'm bleeding."
She rolled her eyes and kept watching her show.
I yelled it again, pleading for her to pay attention.

"Momma, PLEASE! Just be my mom for once and take me to the hospital! I'M SCARED! And I don't know what to do, PLEASE!"

It's as if she has completely turned off her emotions towards me. Even though I know this, I stand and continue to plead with her. She huffed and puffed, but she finally took me.

I hate the emergency room. It makes me want to throw up. They have people who are bleeding out just like me, sit for hours just to get called and then wait another 4 hours to see the doctor. I pray, and I pray that nothing is wrong with my baby, and that I just cut myself or something. Lord please, don't take my heart from me...

****

And I'd give up forever to touch you,
Cause I know that you feel me somehow.
You're the closet to heaven that I'll ever be,
And I don't want to go home right now.
And all I could taste in this moment,

And all I can breathe is your life.

When sooner or later its over…

- Iris
Goo Goo Dolls

****

Chapter 11:

OCTOBER 12TH, 2022

There are good days. Days like today, where I can breathe, where I can shower because I want to and not because I have to. Days where I clean my living room and my bedroom on the same day. Days where I feel OK. Days where I'm not having a heart attack every time a man approaches or sits near me.

Those days seem to go by so quickly. It's like in a flash, they're all gone. And I'm back at the bottom. However, I enjoy them as much as possible. I go shopping, I read books, and I also like to grab some wine and a crap load of popcorn just to sit in my living room and watch Martin re-runs for hours.

Martin is one of my favorite shows. It doesn't matter if I have seen the episode 100 times; I can still laugh at it as if I'm watching it for the first time. My favorite episode is the "*Dead Men Don't Flush*" one where Martin hires a plumber to fix the bathroom, and the group thinks he died. So instead of calling the police, like ordinary people would, they have a fake funeral for him. But at the end, he ends up coming "back to life", because he really wasn't dead to begin with. He just had a disorder that causes him to have pass out spells.

I also like getting my hair done on the days when I feel good. I don't get my hair done often, but on days like this, I not only get my hair retwisted, but I like to get a style too! But there is nothing that I love more than SNACKS.

I LOVE snacks. All different kinds, like: Takis, Skittles, Jolly Ranchers, Chews, etc. On good days, I go Crazy on them! I get all different types of chips and pour them into one bowl, and trust and believe they are GONE before the day ends!

I like these days…
I Love these days.
I NEED these days!

Sometimes, all I need is a break from my own thoughts and feelings, and these days give me that. I'm grateful for that. I don't pretend that these days will last forever. But one day, I hope they are forever…

OCTOBER 15TH, 2011

It's been 3 days...

It's been 3 days since I have eaten.
It's been 3 days since I have showered.

It's been 3 days…
since my baby was taken from me.

And I feel… so… empty…

I still rub my hand over my stomach out of habit;
then I start crying all over again.

SHE'S gone...

I didn't want to know the gender till I gave birth.
And I did give birth… 3 days ago…

My baby just wasn't alive when I did so…

But I decided to still name her…

Espwa…

Espwa means *hope* in Haitian Creole.

She was MY hope.

She gave me purpose when I thought *He* had taken all of mine. I dream and imagine what she would look like if she were here. I would've put her in the cutest clothes and brought her to school. I would have protected her. I would have loved her. I would have been there for her, like I wished my mom was there for me.

I also gave her my dad's last name. He died when I was 6 years old from gang violence. *Etienne.* It means, *crown* or *wealth* in Creole. My mom used to tell me I looked like him. I don't remember him much other than him being around. I wish he was here right now, more than ever.

My mom left me in the hospital. I'm glad she did though. It was already bad enough. I didn't need her Extra negative energy to cloud over me as well. It would've just made it worse.

I remember the day I found out I was pregnant like it was yesterday. The feeling of fear and sadness and pain. I thought that day was the worst day of my life, but I was wrong. The worst day of my life was 3 days ago. The day her life ended.

And in a way, mine did too…

****

I would tell you that I love you tonight,
But I know that I've got time on my side
Where you going? Why you leaving so soon?
Is there somewhere else that's better for you?
What is love, if you're not here with me?
What is love, if it's not guaranteed?
What is love, if it just up and leaves?
What is love, if you're not here no more?
What is love, if you're not really sure?
What is love? What is love…

- What Is Love
V Bozeman

****

Chapter 13:

OCTOBER 15ᵀᴴ, 2022

"Hey Aniyah, I was wondering if I could have you case brief this for me? I will owe you big time." Tuchelianna (*to-che-li-an-na*) is the "it girl" at my job. We don't talk much, but whenever we do, she seems to have good energy. Plus, she really looks like she has herself together. Well, I can't say that, because from the outside I guess I look like I have myself together too.

"Sure, just send over all the paperwork and I will try my best to get to it." She thanks me and starts walking back to her office, but then she stops in her tracks and comes back to my desk.

"Hey, isn't your birthday coming up in a few weeks?" I never celebrate my birthday. The last time I had a birthday party I was 13, so it's been a long time. I was always too scared to be disappointed. So, I never asked for anything.

"Yeah, it is. I'm not really doing anything though."
She frowns.

"Girl, you HAVE to celebrate your 26th birthday!
Why don't you let me take you to Bougies! It's a
lounge downtown. Get out for once and have some
fun! You only turn 26 once. Why not do it big!?
You down?"

In my mind, I'm screaming, I don't want to
celebrate. I don't want to celebrate. I don't want to
celebrate! To me, turning 26 isn't that big of a deal.
It's just an in between year. But, I get that she's
trying to be nice, so I shouldn't turn her down.
Right?

"Um… Sure… Just, not a lot of people, ok? I'm not
really good with crowds." She agrees and goes into
her office, and I instantly regret my decision.
Why did I say yes? What would I wear? What
would I say? She's probably going to cancel
anyway though, so I guess I shouldn't get too
worked up. Right?

When I got home, I pulled out my red box where I keep the tapes of my dad. This is probably the closest thing to a tradition that I have. I watch his tapes every year, usually close to my birthday and on his. After I finished watching all of them, I grabbed a glass of wine, ate a brownie and went to sleep.

Chapter 14:

November 7th, 2011

"Happy Birthday Aniyah! Your grandma said check the mail, she sent you some money!" That was the nicest thing my mom has said to me in a very long time. I really don't want to celebrate my birthday this year. I barely want to get up. *Espwa* would have been one month old. I had planned to just take the bus and go downtown to see a show or something, but seeing as she is not here, there is no reason for me to celebrate anything.

I'm 16 today. My grief time is almost over. This is my last week before I could not only lose my job, but I could get dropped from school. I'm not ready to go back yet. I just want to stay in this little bubble and never face anything again. But I have to. I still have to try to be someone. Someone that *Espwa* could be proud of.

I go to the mailbox and see this big package with my name on it, along with my grandma's gift. It says it's from my dad. That can't be possible. My dad is dead. I run and take it to my room. I open it quietly, so my mom doesn't hear.

It's a box. A red box with black permanent marker writing that says, "*If you turn 16 and I'm not there*". Wow... he left me something? Why? What is it? I open the box, and it is a bunch of tape recordings. There's also something to play them on. After a while, I figured out how to put the recordings in the music box thing, and I hit play. It's my dad spitting poetry! I never thought my dad could be a poet! I mean, I guess I could believe it. Tupac was a gangster and one of the best poets of all time.

My dad was a Vik Nine. He and my mom had me at 17, and he joined it then. He was on the sidewalk one day, with a group of other VN's, and suddenly, a car came down the block and shot out the window. They tried to run, but my dad just wasn't fast enough. I wish he would have run fast enough...

****

Close your eyes,

Have no fear.

The monster's gone,

He's on the run and your daddy's here.

Beautiful, beautiful, beautiful

Beautiful boy...

- Beautiful Boy (Darling Boy)
John Lennon

****

Part 2:

"The Poking"

Chapter 15:

November 7th, 2022

Today is my 26th birthday, and I'm actually doing something. I haven't celebrated my birthday in over 10 years. I never thought I would ever celebrate again. Even though I've never been a huge "party" person, I can appreciate Tuchelianna wanting to do something kind for me. She didn't have to. I still haven't found anything to wear, and I don't want to embarrass myself by wearing something terrible. So I text Tuchelianna to try and cancel because I can't find anything.

Me: Hey, could we put a rain check on tonight?

I can't find anything birthday appropriate.

Tuchelianna: Um, No!

Send me your address.

I'll pick you up! Let's go shopping!

Me: Wait…What?

Tuchelianna: Just count it as a part of your birthday gift from me!

Me: Are you sure? It's really not necessary.

Tuchelianna: Girl, YES!

We are turning UP tonight!

PERIOOOOOD!

Me: Um, ok…

1946 Graceworthy Blvd.

That's my address.

Tuchelianna: Ok! Be there in few hours!

She gets here at 5:30 P.M., and her car is Nice. It smells like mango and pomegranate, an odd mix I would think, but it goes together so well! I hope I don't say anything stupid or awkward and run her away.

"Hey Birthday Girl! How are you?" she says with a smile that could quite literally blind the darkness with the amount of light in it.

"I'm ok, just turned 26 and don't know how to feel; I'm guess I'm getting old!" I say with a laugh. When I said that, I realized something. I'm Almost 30. All these years I've been on this earth, even though I feel like I haven't lived at all. It's as if I've been in one of those time capsule things from *Black Lightning*, where I'm technically alive but not really living.

"Girl, you still got a lot of living to do! Enjoy it! I live every day like it's my last, and I don't apologize for it either. Especially as black women. We often feel we have to supply everyone else with happiness, even if that means we don't have any left to supply for ourselves. I refuse to live like that!"

Wow... That makes a lot of sense. Maybe that's why she carries herself as though she's on top of the world, because to her, she IS...

"I never looked at it like that. Look at you, dropping gems. Ok girl, I see you!" I say as she pulls into the mall. I've never been to this one. I always went to a different mall with my grandma in Chicago when I was little, before she got sick. I used to get in the little fake kids' cars where you could turn the wheel, and your parents would push you. It was fun being that age with no cares, no worries and no fears; other than getting coal for Christmas if you were being bad.

I wonder what my life would've been like if *Espwa* was still here. I would've put her in one of those little cars and driven her around the mall all day. I would have bought her all the clothes in the store and come home with 900 bags of bows and barrettes!

"Let's go into this store! They have cute stuff in here!", she says while directing me into this humongous clothing store. Looks like it should be in LA! You can tell everyone goes here for prom and wedding dresses. I would have never come in here on my own though. I hate dresses, I always have. I don't know why, but I prefer jumpsuits or pantsuits any day. So seeing all of these pretty dresses instantly makes me feel like I'm in the wrong store.

"Hey, how can I help you, ladies today?", a girl with locs like mine says. But hers are ginger and goes down to her butt, breaking rule #10.

"Uh, yea. It's my birthday, and I wanted something cute to wear. Do you have anything black?" The girl smiles, then directs us to the private dressing area. She gives us a glass of champagne while we wait for her to bring some options.

While we're waiting, Tuchelianna says with a curious look, "So, why didn't you want to celebrate your birthday?" I sigh, because I really don't want to tell her why. I'm not quite ready to open up. I don't want her perception of me to change. I don't want sympathy, but I know I need a friend.

Hesitantly, I reply, "Well, I didn't have a lot of support growing up, so I just never really celebrated my birthday." Of course I'm not telling too much. Just enough for her to understand.

"Everyone deserves to celebrate their birthday! As I said, we deserve happiness too. We're human just like everyone else." I just sigh and sit quietly until the worker returns with the dresses, and thankfully Tuchelianna doesn't push me for a response. She just sits there with me.

"Hello again ladies! Ok, I found 5 dresses I think you will like. Let me help you try them on!" She takes me into the little side room to change. I hate looking at my body in the *mirror*. I close my eyes as she puts the dress on me and takes me outside.

"OMG! Girl, you look GOOOOD! Do you like it?" Tuchelianna shouted. I open my eyes, and I don't see what she sees. It's not like I hate the dress, I just hate the way I look in the dress.

"What's wrong? Do you not like it?" she says with a confused demeanor.

"It's not that I Don't like it, but I don't feel like it looks good on Me."

"You look Amazing. Don't sweat it!" The worker says with a smile. I stare at the champagne we left on the table as I think. This dress breaks rule #13. No tight or short-cut dresses. It's tight Everywhere and barely passes the middle of my thigh. I Wanna say no, but then I think, if I was tainted without the dress, what difference would it really make?

After a big exhale, I say, "Ok, we will take this one. How much is it?" The worker pulls the tag to look at the price. Before she tells me the price, I walk toward the table to grab my purse. "It is $750, so it will be about $760 with taxes. Is that fine?" She questioned.

Tuchelianna interjects "Yes! That's fine. I will pay upfront with a card."

"Are you sure? That is a lot of money, don't feel like you have to spend that on me. You are already paying for the lounge. I can pay, or we can split it." She rolls her eyes, laughs at me, and tells me, she is sure. I still feel bad though. No one has Ever spent that much money on me. She pays, I thank her, and we leave to head to the lounge.

It is so beautiful on the inside. It has chandeliers and marble floors and a huge dance floor. When we got to our private party room, I saw almost everyone from work and almost threw up. There is a cake table on one side, and on the other side is a gift table, and it is full of gifts. More gifts than I have ever gotten in my life. I started to cry and laugh simultaneously, overwhelmed by the number of people that showed up. People began approaching me and hugging me, telling me how beautiful I looked. All I can do is smile from ear to ear. This time, it is a Real smile. Because for once, I am Really happy...

Chapter 16:

JANUARY 18TH, 2012
THE LAST FLASHBACK...

People whisper at school. People stare and point. One day I was pregnant, and the next, I was not, yet there is no baby. People spread rumors like:

"...she gave it up for adoption..."
"...the baby daddy made her give it to him..."
"...she left it at the hospital and ran away..."
"...she had drugs in her system, so they took it..."

I bet they would all feel stupid if they knew what really happened. But I never correct them. Why would I? I probably deserve the name-calling and whispers anyway, since I couldn't keep her alive. The fact of the matter is, I Failed Her. And I will probably never forgive myself for it.

When I'm in school, I don't look up. I look down and walk fast. I don't raise my hand. I don't speak. I don't try out for sports. I don't sign up for activities. I just show up and do my work. That's it. In fact, I give my Best work. Because I have to, for *her*. Even with all the whispers and rumors, even though I don't participate, I still want to come to school. Not to talk to anyone, but to escape. At school, I don't have to hear my mom's mouth or see all the unopened baby products I will never use. My brother asked me if I was going to donate them, but I don't think I can. I can't let it go. It's like I was letting *her* go.

"Mrs. Aniyah, if you could pay attention, that would be great." My math teacher says in an annoyed tone.

"I'm sorry Mrs. Basura." I hope she just moves on.

"I know you just had your baby a few months ago, but school must also be your priority." I am completely taken back by what she said. What makes her think that school comes even close to the responsibility or importance of having a baby!?

"OK Mrs. Basura. Can you please continue…"
The rest of the class just watches as she rolls her eyes. And instead of just continuing with her class, she decides to keep going.

"I really don't understand what it is with you young girls and having babies. It's really ridiculous."
Every part of my body starts to burn and itch with aggravation…. WHO does she think she is! As if she knows every situation.

"Yeah, and I don't know what it is with these young boys putting the babies in us either. But I guess we will never know, huh...." I reply as I shrug and slouch back in my chair. That didn't make me feel better, but I guess it made the rest of the class feel better because they all started laughing hysterically. I've never been the type to disrespect a teacher. However, her comment was incredibly inappropriate, and she embarrassed me in front of the entire class. I may be a child, but there is only so much a child can take.

"Excuse me, but that attitude is unnecessary and really insulting, so I would like you to meet me after class today for a little chat with your mom." She thinks that that was supposed to upset or scare me? Please, my mom probably won't even answer the phone, let alone do anything about what "disrespect" she felt I gave her.

One thing about my mom is, she really doesn't trip about school. I don't know if it's because she doesn't care about Me or just doesn't care about School, but she has never been to one of my parent teachers' conferences, and any time a teacher calls about my behavior, which is rare, she never does anything about it. Not even yell at me. Most of the time, I would have to sign my own field trip forms, write my own absence note AND give myself early dismissals. Honestly, that I am grateful for.

Chapter 17:

January 18th, 2023

I never had a lot of friends growing up.
And most of the ones I did have, left when I got
pregnant. They didn't know why I was pregnant,
because I didn't feel like I should have to tell them.
Plus, you know, what happens in the house Stays in
the house. Right? That's a whole 'nother rule.

Due to that, I was understandably nervous about
building a friendship with Tuchelianna. To be
honest, I still am…. But she has so far proven to be
pretty legit. Though I never fully trust anyone 100%
because there's Always a chance for them to hurt
me. I mean, if you can't trust your Mom 100%, can
you Really trust Anybody?

Anyway, we were supposed to meet for drinks at
8 P.M., but I'm trying to finish up this last piece of
paperwork before court tomorrow, so I will
probably have to rush to get ready. I've gone out

more in these last couple of months th3an in the last decade. And you know what, it's actually been fun. It's so liberating, being able to enjoy these moments without guilt or outside stress.

I hop in the shower, scorching hot per usual, and put on this black jumpsuit that I think I got off Shein. We get to the bar, I order a strawberry margarita, she gets a watermelon one, and we just sit and sip on that for a bit while we talk.

"It's crazy how we've been friends for a minute, but I still feel like I don't know much about you!" she says with a questioning smile.

This is what I was afraid of. What if I let her get too close? I don't want a sympathy friend. I Really don't want a sympathy friend.

"Yeah, I don't really talk about myself a lot...
Um, I grew up in Chicago...
I have a younger brother...

I majored in business management as an undergrad, but I did a dual degree, so I have my master's in business administration as well.
My favorite color is black.
Aaaand… I LOVE Martin!"

She laughs out loud when I say, "I love Martin".

"OMG, I love Martin too! But, unpopular opinion, I cannot STAND Gina!" We both laugh together. We laugh so loud that people stare, but they assume we're drunk, so they don't say anything.

Tuchelianna continues to make her point, "She wines Entirely too much for me. I can't take it! She acts like she's 4 years old." Our laughter is pure and bounces off the walls, which interestingly enough creates this invisible breeze that makes me feel light and at ease…

"Girl, these margaritas are about to make me cancel my therapy appointment in the morning! It's at 7:30 A.M. I might just use that time to Sleep before work," she said with a chuckle.

"Therapy? You go to therapy?" I said, puzzled. I never went to therapy. Though I probably should have. We were taught that therapy was for crazy people. And Black people don't do therapy.

"Yeah, I've been going since I started law school. I wouldn't have survived without it. I know in our community we shy away from it, but I promise it's actually very beneficial. You should try it!"

"I don't know, I don't think sitting on someone's couch talking about my feelings will fix My mess."

"Don't knock it till you've tried it! You don't have to sit on a couch in real life. That's really just on tv. I use a program called Greater Help. It's only online or in person, and you can pick out a therapist based on your personal needs and preferences."

"What if it doesn't work? What if they judge me?"

"They can't judge you. It's against their rules. Give it a try! I'm sure you'll like it."

I don't know. I'm not ready for therapy. I cannot begin to unwarp the mess that is my life because if I start, I might just totally come undone. I might never be able to assemble myself again! Just like Humpty Dumpty...

"Well, I'm gonna get going because I actually have Martin reruns to watch, but it was nice catching up with you! We have to do this again soon," I say as I grab my purse. We hug and walk towards the door and then to our cars.

That therapy conversation threw me for a loop! I couldn't focus on whatever she was saying because it stuck in my mind. So, I left early. I return to my house, throw my purse, and almost run to the fridge for a bottle of anything stronger than a margarita. When I'm finished drinking, I go to my room and pray that my brain remembers everything it needs for court tomorrow.

Chapter 18:

JANUARY 19TH, 2023

Today is court day, and I regret those margaritas and those two Additional shots of Tequila. I stopped getting hung over a long time ago, after I think my 10th Jack bottle run-through back in law school. I think my body had gotten accustomed to the poison I was putting inside of it. But today was different. My head was banging like a marching band bass drum was going BOOM! BOOM! BOOM! on my brain...

I searched my apartment for Ibuprofen, but I couldn't find any. I search for Excedrin, but again, nothing. The moment I need something, it's never there! At this point, I don't know What to do. There is no way I can sit in court for hours with no medicine with this momentous headache.

I turn to Google and ask what I can do for a hangover if I don't have any medication. They say to drink tea. I don't have tea. They say to drink coffee. And go figure, I don't have coffee. Wine is my tea, and Jack is my coffee, and those will only make it worse. SO, my final option is to run to the corner store, which will make me late for court. But at least I won't throw up in the middle of my opening arguments due to my headache!

It never fails, the corner store is packed. It NEVER fails, and really, it's not packed. It's just that they only use one cashier per store. So, the 8 people who decided to go grocery shopping at the corner store this morning is in One Line. I grab some extra fast relief Excedrin, and I get in line. By the time I get to the front of it, it's already 11:55 A.M. Court starts at 12:15 P.M. I was already going to be late, but Now I'm going to be even LATER!

I panic trying to get out of this store in time, so I end up tripping myself, and I fall into a puddle of water, messing up my clothes. The one time I wear my fancy blazer, it gets ruined. I run back into the store to see if they have some paper towels to help wipe the muddy water off me. I get dry, but now I'm all muddy and gross. Great…

I pay more attention to my surroundings as I leave the store for the second time. I check the time in my car. It's now 12:10 P.M. I am never this behind. I can't believe I allowed myself to be this clumsy and stupid. I just pray the judge doesn't notice and that everybody is running behind and not just me...

Of course my prayer didn't work…
When I arrived, it was 12:30 P.M. My client was waiting out in the hall, and she was heated.

"Um, hello, you were supposed to be here 15 minutes ago! How inconsiderate can you be? What if the jury thinks bad of me because of this? You could really mess my chances up! Do you know that? I bet you don't know because you're incompetent! I don't know why I hired you. Your people can never be on time."

Now, I've always had to deal with racism, and I've always ignored it. But not today, today I have time.

"First, what do you mean by 'my people'. As you can see from my outfit, there was an incident that made me late, and yes, that is on me. However, I have 3 degrees, and you have a middle school diploma, so PLEASE, try me Not with the 'incompetent' comments. And I would tread lightly with someone who has your freedom in her hands, so 'my people' that." All of which I said in my full Olivia Pope voice. I know it was my fault for not being here on time, but racism is Never ok. THAT I know.

"How dare you speak to me that way. You're fired! And I will Not be paying you." she said, pointing her finger in my face. And if there are any rules on talking to black people, you never, EVER put your finger in their face. Because to US, that's a gesture that makes us think you want to fight.

I take a giant deep breath... And when I take a deep breath, I swallow all of the angry words that are trying so hard to escape my lips... I also swallowed all those hands that were about to be thrown.

"You can't fire me, because I Quit! Also, you signed an hourly contract, so I will be billing you for the hours until now. If you decide to refuse payment, I guess I will STILL be seeing you here in court."

Then, I just walked off. Not caring one bit about whatever she had to say back...

Part 3:

"The Awakening"

Chapter 19:

January 20th, 2023

I stare at my wall and question my life...
I question the moon and the stars. I question the
earth and its rotation. I question everything.
Why am I here? What purpose do I serve? Am I just
a placeholder for someone more important? I pay
close attention to my breath and the rate of my
heartbeat. I try to control it. I take it out of the
ordinary, and when I try to give it back, it won't
accept it, and I freak out.

My mouth gets dry.

The room spins.

I panic.

Is this where it all ends?

Is this really it for me!?

I gasp, trying to cling to the air as a mountain
climber to a mountain. What is this? I have never
felt this before. It's as if the air is taking revenge on
me for humans polluting it. Then everything just

stops. My heart starts to beat normally again, and once the room stops spinning, I like any human, I rushed to Google to see what just happened to me. Google gives me three possible reasons:

1. I had a panic attack.
2. I had a mini-stroke.
3. I died.

I don't know how they came up with the last one because if I was dead, I wouldn't need Google to tell me that. So, I assume it was probably number 1. I don't understand why, though. I've never had one before. Why now? Google then leads me to resources like medicines and vitamins. I can try to lower the percentage of it happening again. Google also directs me to Greater Help. The therapy site Tuchelianna was telling me about. It's 24/7, and it's all virtual. It says I can pick my own therapist. I don't trust it…

What if the therapist reports me to a crazy house once I open up?

What if they can't help me?

What if I'm unfixable!?

My heart races again, my lungs swell, and the room starts spinning like a fast carousel. I can't breathe. I try to focus. If I can get out of this once, I can do it again, right? I try to get off my bed and get to my desk so it can help me to stand straight. I trip. My heart beats faster, the room spins faster, faster, faster, and faster, then it stops again...

Everything starts working normally like nothing ever happened. I can't keep living like this. I have no choice but to take my chances with these Greater Help people. So, I go to their sign-up page.

They make me answer all these questions like: **How would you rate your mental health on a scale of 1-10? 1 being horrible and 10 being outstanding.**

I answer them as honestly as I can, and they give me a list of therapists they assume will best suit me. Most of them are white, old, and just creepy looking. I keep scrolling until I see Dr. Miller. She's black, and she is older but not too old. She has a lot of experience as well, so I click on her profile. It says I can message her to schedule a meeting.

So I do. I introduced myself simply and asked when she was available. She responds promptly and says she has an opening at 4:30 P.M. That's this afternoon. That's only three hours away! I started to feel rushed, and scared, and overwhelmed. Think Aniyah. Think. Think. Think. You need this. You need her. I reluctantly accept her opening, and she looks forward to seeing me soon. I close my laptop and jump in the shower.

I start to think about how this session is going to go. What if I just cancel it? Give myself more time before I just jump in. I tell myself No. You need to do this today. It's 3:30 P.M., and I'm in my robe, watching the clock tik.

       Watching... aaand watching...

       Waiting... aaand waiting....

The minutes went by so slowly, or at least they seemed to. Then the next thing I knew, it was 4:15 P.M., and I was still in my robe. I can't go to therapy in a robe. What if I just turn off my camera? No, Aniyah! That's unprofessional.

So, I grab a random pair of joggers and t-shirt, and a
bra and sit at my desk.

4:25 P.M...

4:26 P.M...

4:27 P.M...

4:28 P.M...

I click the Zoom link she gave me for when it's
time, and I wait...

4:29 P.M...

4:30 P.M...

She's not here yet. Is she still coming? Aniyah, stop
worrying so much. It's barely 4:30 P.M. RELAX...

4:31 P.M...

4:32 P.M...

4:33 P.M...

4:34 P.M...

4:35 P.M...

She finally joins, with a smile. I sit up straight.

"Hello there! I'm sorry I'm late. My other meeting
kind of went over a bit. My name is Dr. Miller.
I have been a therapist for about 10 years.

How about you? Tell me about yourself!"

I gulp and take a deep breath.

"Um… My name is Aniyah… I'm 25… I grew up in Chicago and moved to Atlanta for work. I work in Big Law…."

She smiles. "Nice, I grew up in the Chi as well! What side did you grow up on?" Because that's what EVERY Chicagoan asks when someone says they're from Chicago. Her voice was smooth and comforting. Like a grandmother telling you a different bedtime story because you couldn't sleep.

"Westside mostly, but sometimes I stayed with my grandma on the southside." So far, this seems normal. I don't sense anything off putting about her. But of course it's still too early to draw any conclusions.

"So, what made you want to start therapy?" she asked as she grabbed a pen off her desk in front of her and the notebook next to it.

"Well, I had two of these bizarre and scary experiences earlier, and when I looked it up, google said it was a panic attack, and then it directed me to your company's site." I began to fiddle with my fingers, trying not to get nervous.

"Ok! Can you tell me about these experiences?" she said as she began taking notes in her notebook. "And also, before you answer, you seem new to this, so I just wanted to let you know that anything you disclose to me is purely confidential unless you disclose that you are going to harm yourselves or others. Ok?" she says reassuringly.

"Ok, that's good because that was something I was going to ask you about. And what happened was that I was thinking about stuff. Then my heart started beating about a trillion miles per hour, and the room felt like it was running a marathon with how fast it was spinning. I felt like I was chasing my breath. Then it just stopped."

"And how did those experiences make you feel?"
She said and then stopped writing to listen to my
response.

"It made me feel scared and confused because I'd
never had one of those before. Which I'm actually
surprised I haven't had one way before now. I
thought I was dying."

"Those feelings and thoughts are understandable
and valid." she said with a comforting smile.
This was probably one of the first times someone
validated my feelings and told me that I was ok to
feel the way I felt. It feels so different. I'm used to
academic validation, seeing as I've always managed
to do well in school. But this emotional validation
feels warm and like a breath of relief.

"Now, let's talk more about what led up to those
panic attacks. You said you were thinking about
some things. What things were you thinking
about?" she asked calmly.

The warm feeling, I was feeling two seconds ago was just replaced by a new cold and icy one...
That new feeling is fear. I can answer without letting her in too much, right?

"Um, I was just thinking about life, work, and stuff like that," I said, forcing myself to sit up straight and look at her so she couldn't see that I was withholding the true depth of my thoughts.

"Ok, and what about life and work stressed you out to the point where you had a panic attack?" she asks, continuing to write in her notebook.

I shrug my shoulders. I say nothing. I just shrug...

"Well, I can only help you if you help me. I need to know what about life and work is having you so stressed so that we can better explain and deal with your panic attacks. And try to prevent them from happening in the future."

I don't know what to say. Where do I start? How do I begin to try and unpack this suitcase so filled with worries?

"I was thinking about why I'm here and not someone else... I was thinking about my purpose." I say as I shake my leg up and down, which I do when I am uncomfortable.

"Ok, and what made you start to question that?" she asks, while looking at her notebook and continuously writing and writing.

"I don't know, it just kind of popped up out of nowhere," I say, looking down at my hands.
She stops writing, folds her hands, and looks at me deeply.

"Well, it seems like these thoughts are most likely your insecurities trying to get to you. Next session, we can focus on breaking those insecurities down and creating some long-term coping skills to deal with these 'pop-ups.' But until then, if this happens again, wherever you are, I want you to stop, look around, and try to find:

> 5 things you can see
>
> 4 things you can feel
>
> 3 things you can hear

2 things you can smell

and 1 thing that you Know...

This method should help you calm down."

She grabs her notebook and puts it in a drawer

along with the pen.

"Thank you. Today's meeting wasn't as bad as I

thought it would be. It was hard, but not bad." I say

with a slight smile.

She smiles back. "I'm glad. Should I schedule you

for my next open availability?"

"Sure, that's fine." I say, tapping on a pad of sticky

notes near me.

"Ok, great, my next opening is Friday at 12:30 P.M.

Does that work for you? "

"Yes, that works fine. Thank you again."

"No problem, take care. And I will see you next

week!" She says as she waves and ends the call.

This was a lot less scary than I imagined, but still

difficult. And even though I didn't share much,

I was still drained. So I took my clothes off, put back on my robe, hopped in the bed, closed my eyes, and fell asleep…

Chapter 20:

February 4th, 2023

It's been a couple of weeks since my first therapy appointment. I haven't told anybody that I go yet. I don't want anybody to know. I don't want to be judged or people to think I'm crazy. I hate to say it, but I like it; even though I know I shouldn't. We haven't talked about anything deep or significant, yet. I'm still trying to trust her before I really let her in. My next session is today at 5 P.M. Even though we don't talk about the hard stuff, telling somebody about my day feels good.

No interrupting, no criticizing, just listening.

I told her about the racist client I had. I even told her exactly what I said back. And she didn't even judge my response; she just LISTENED…

I also made dinner for the first time in forever. I made chicken and rice. It was a simple meal, but it was really good. I sat at my dinner table, and instead of wine, I had cranberry juice in a wine glass. It's close enough, I guess.

I turned on the tv, and I put on Martin. This is the episode where Martin has to go to a high school reunion. Gina had an allergic reaction, and her face was all messed up. Before I know it, it's 4:50 P.M., and I need to hop on Zoom for my virtual therapy session. I wait for her. 4:50 P.M.... 4:51 P.M.... 4:53 P.M.... 4:54 P.M.... PING! She joins the call with the same notepad and pencil she brings to every meeting. She's been early ever since the first meeting.

She greets me and asks me the basics; and I answer her, telling her about me cooking for the first time in years and how good it was. I told her about Martin, and I told her about the cranberry juice.

"Why did you need to put your cranberry juice in a wine glass." she asks, curiously. Before I even start to answer, she starts writing in her notepad.

"I like to drink wine… a lot…. and I wanted to do something different without it actually looking like I'm doing something different, I guess." I never looked up from my desk. I mean, technically I'm not lying. I DO like wine. And I DID want to do something different. So, why does it still feel like I'm lying?

She proceeds to say, "Is that the real reason, or do you struggle with alcohol?" Well… I guess this is where it begins… It's as if she is literally staring into my soul. I try not to look her in the eyes, so instead, I put my eyes back on my desk and pretend to be fixing a piece of split wood.

"Aniyah, I know we haven't touched on certain issues these past few sessions, but I think it's time we got to the root of your panic attacks. So, I'm going to ask you again, do you have a problem with alcohol?" My legs start to shake, and my heart starts to beat fast. Something that I thought was just a simple statement has become bigger than I expected. I'm not ready to get bigger yet. I'm not ready to peel off my band-aid.

I replied with a little bit of audacity and still not quite looking at her, "I don't have a '*problem*' with alcohol. I just like it a lot. And I'm '*trying*' to make some different lifestyle choices. So I'm just working on slowing down on it, a little bit."

She reaches into her drawer, pulls out a ball with small squishy balls inside, places it in front of her, and takes a deep breath.

"This is a stress ball. This ball is what I use when I'm stressed to calm down, but also to change my focus off what is bothering me by focusing on the balls inside. This is what I'm guessing you do with your wine. Am I correct?" She then picks up the ball and begins to squish it.

A bit taken back, I reply, "I mean, it helps. I don't think that's a bad thing. It's a *fix*." I say, while looking at my hands. I twist them around each other, and as I do when I'm anxious. Then I realize I need lotion.

"Do you really think that alcohol will 'fix' your problems?" she asked me.

I shrug my shoulders as I reply, "Well, I didn't say 'It' fixes my problems. I said, it's a *fix*." I continue to fiddle with my dry hands.

She starts to write in her notepad again for what seems like forever.

Getting a little nervous I try to fix up my last statement, "I mean, like I said, it helps. So yeah..." I say, doubting my own thoughts. I wish we could drop this topic and move on to something else.

"Ok... well, do you know that using alcohol to solve your problems is not healthy? Because at that point, all you would be doing is masking the pain of whatever you're going through. And there is only so much masking you can do before you finally can't mask anymore. It could quite literally cause you to mentally and emotionally fall apart."

I don't want to talk about this. I don't need to hear this right now. "Well, I thank you for your time! I have soooo many cases to go over for work, so unfortunately, I will have to cut this session short. Same time next week?" I ask, trying my best not to break.

She smiles solemnly at me... "Ok Aniyah, that's fine. We will pick this discussion back up during our next session. Enjoy the rest of your week." She says as she puts the ball and notepad back in her desk. I nod and log off the session.

My heart is pounding as her words keep repeatedly playing in my head like a skipping CD. This is too much. My hands start to sweat... the room starts spinning again... and my heart feels like it's out of my chest. I gasp for air, as if I just got out of a marathon. I stumble my way into the kitchen and start searching for a *fix*. Brandy, Jack, Robitussin, ANYTHING! Just something to calm me down.

In the back of my fridge, I see half a bottle of Jack. I don't even grab a glass. I am drowning. Suffocating. With every sip I take, it gives me just enough weight to float above the water...

The water of her voice finally leaves my ears...

And now, it's quiet...

Very quiet...

My *fix*...

Chapter 21:

February 14th, 2023

Today, is love day. The day when couples
can have 5-hour make-out sessions in the middle of
a store, and no one says anything because it's love
day. The day when people celebrate a fat fake angel
who shoots darts at people that makes them fall in
love. When it comes to me, today is just the day I
shove my mouth with 10 pounds of discounted
candy, sit on a couch, and watch Highschool
Musical for the 90th thousandth time.

I'm in the middle of the movie when,
I get a text. It's from my therapist. I ignore it.
I get an email. It's from my therapist. I ignore it.
It's been 10 days since we talked. I skipped my last
appointment. I don't need it. I know what works.
My *fix* works. No need to fix what isn't broken…

Is it broken?

No Aniyah, you're fine.

Right! I Am FINE!

As I'm thinking about my fix, I realize I don't have anymore. I stand up, and my stomach turns. I don't feel so good. I've been having stomach pain for the past couple of days. But I just figure it's a sign for me to go to the store to get what puts all my pain to sleep. My *fix*.

When I'm on my way to the store, my stomach gets worse. It feels like it's being ripped apart by something. I press on the gas a little harder; I need to get to my *fix*. I run towards the Jack. And of course, with my luck, they don't have anymore. So I grab the next best thing....

"Hello Whiskey..." I haven't had you since law school, but I need my fix. So, I grab two bottles, but this time I run to self-checkout. I pay, and then I run to the car. Before I even lock the door, I open the bottle, and I drink. I down not even half bottle before I throw it right back up. I can't control it.

It's Everywhere… On my steering wheel, my face, and my clothes. I don't know what to do. I can barely open my eyes. I force myself to open the door to ask for help. I fall out of the car onto the ground and try to scream, but nothing comes out. The whole world starts spinning, and my heart begins to beat slowly.

Then everything…

just goes…

dark...

Chapter 22:

February 16th, 2023

I have been in the hospital for 2 days. Someone eventually came out of Benny's, saw me on the ground covered in vomit, and called 911. Obviously not one of my best moments. I don't really know who or when they found me because I was still blacked out. All I remember is what happened before I passed out, and what's happening now. I've been going in and out of consciousness, and my head is pounding. All I can hear is the constant agonizing beep of the machine connected to my arm through the IV. Every time the doctor has come to do check-ins, I've been sleeping. I try to keep my eyes open long enough to see the doctor, but the beeping and the tumultuous headache make me want to jump off a roof.

I look around the room to try and find my phone. I need to call my job. I've been off the grid for two days now. I know I'm behind on work, and I have court tomorrow. I have to get out of this hospital. As I think about how deep I am in work, my heart starts to beat fast. Faster and faster, it beats as if it's going to explode if I don't get my briefcase in my hand in 3.8 seconds. Within the next moment, a nurse walks into the room armed with a stethoscope and a tray full of needles and medicine.

"Everything is OK Ms. Aniyah. I'm going to help you sit up. Just try to take a deep breath for me, ok?" she says as she pulls her stethoscope from around her neck and puts it behind my back. She mimics the deep breath she wants me to take as she moves the stethoscope around my back, checking my pulse. I get out about 4 deep breaths before the room starts to slow down, along with my heartrate.

"See, you are OK. You're safe. Would you like some water?" she says as she walks over to the water machine in the room.

"What happened to me?" I ask with a scratchy, raspy voice.

"What happened right now, or what got you here?" she asked calmly while checking her watch and writing something down on a clipboard.

"Why am I here? What brought me here?" I say as I begin to cough. Only to suddenly realize there's blood is in my hand from when I coughed! Not a lot, but enough to freak me out. The nurse comes over, sees the blood, and tells me she will be right back as she goes to get the doctor. Now I'm really freaking out, because not only do I not know why I'm here, but now I'm coughing up blood. I'm scared. I haven't been this scared since I lost my *Espwa*.

The doctor comes in with the same clipboard the nurse had, with an urgent and dignified look on his face like he is solving a crime. He checked my vitals silently. He stared at me, still not saying a word. He moved around me like I was merely a statue he was putting the final touches on.
The silence is killing me. I need to know what is happening, and I need to know now!

"Can you please tell me what's wrong with me!?
First, I'm blacking out in the middle of Benny's
parking lot, and now I'm coughing up blood." I say,
pleading with him for the information they are
seemingly hiding from me.

"You are suffering from **AWS** which is *alcohol
withdrawal syndrome*. You were brought here
because you were found lying on the ground in
shock due to alcohol poisoning. If the person who
called 911 would have gotten to you even a minute
later, you would have likely either died or had a
major loss like part of your liver or a kidney..."
the doctor explained with a sorrowful tone.

I almost died? I almost DIED! Like died for real.
Not panic attack dying or Hannah Baker joke type
of dying. I almost died from my fix. The thing that
was supposed to stop me from Wanting to die
almost killed me... I don't believe it. There is no
way. I would have felt like I should stop before
now. I had control. Did I have control? I start to sob
uncontrollably. How could I do this to myself?

How could I let it get this bad? It was just a fix; I didn't do this on purpose...

I began to cry small rivers. The doctor grabs tissue off the desk close to the door and hands it to me. I cry into them, soaking them, hoping that if I cry enough, I could cry myself out of this nightmare. That I would wipe my eyes and wake up to this all being a bad dream, and that my *fix* worked, just like it always has.

"We think you may benefit from attending an outpatient rehab facility and speaking to a therapist. Do you already have a therapist that you can call?" he said while handing me medicine to help stop the symptoms.

Rehab? What makes him think I need rehab? I'm not an alcoholic. I just got a little carried away, that's all.

"I don't need rehab. I'm fine. I can stop whenever I want to." I said as I tried to sit up in the bed. That was a bad idea because the moment my back hit the pillow after I adjusted myself, my stomach adjusted itself all over the room floor. It just kept going and going and going. The doctor ran to grab a throw-up bucket and placed it under my head. When my stomach was finally satisfied, the doctor called for someone to clean up the mess.

"The vomiting and the blacking out seem to prove otherwise. You need help, Aniyah. If you don't get help now, you Will die. You can't fight alcoholism on your own. I will bring psych down here in an hour to talk to you. After 48 hours of observation, you will be discharged. From there, you can choose whether you die when you walk out of here, or live. It's up to you..." He leaves and closes the door behind him.

Now I'm stuck in here, stuck with these choices, these feelings and this ultimatum… I stare at the wall with my thoughts overflowing. The first thing my mind thinks to do is grab a bottle of Jack so that I can fall asleep. However, unfortunately, I don't have that here. So I just keep staring and staring, until the psychiatrist comes in with an even bigger clipboard and long, naturally curly hair in a ponytail. She looks serious; there isn't even a hint of a smile on her face. There is "Truth" written all over her. She looks like she will tell you what you need to hear, and not just what you want to hear. I guess I need that… I just don't really WANT it...

"Hello, Aniyah, I am Dr. Gerizon. How are we feeling right now?" she asked, while still not smiling. She pulled out the doctor's chair from the desk to sit in, rolled it in front of my bed, crossed her legs, and placed her clipboard on top as she proceeded to await my response.

"Well, I'm in the hospital talking to a psychiatrist, so as good as I can be I guess." I said irritably, wanting to rip this beeping machine out of the wall and throw it off the Empire State Building!

"Well then, let's talk about WHY you're in the hospital. What happened? " when she speaks, she takes a lot of pauses. She chooses her words carefully. Like she's picking a space in the word to buy a vowel in Wheel of Fortune. I stall answering her question by readjusting myself on the bed, slower this time. However, knowing she won't let it go, I suck it up, release a big sigh, and answer.

"I was in a Benny's parking lot, and I started drinking. The next thing I know, I'm spilling out of the car, and then in the hospital."

"Ok. Well when did you First start drinking? How old were you?" the doctor replied.

"I started drinking the freshman year of undergrad at parties and stuff." She sighs understandingly, which is probably the most emotion I have seen her express this whole time.

"Ok. So, when you were drinking in your first year of undergrad, it was isolated just at the parties?" I nod my head yes. She writes in her notepad while the machine beeps… and beeps… and beeps… Driving me INSANE!

"So, when did drinking become a regular occurrence for you?" she asked as I continued to lose my mind. My head was already pounding from the beep machine, NOW the intercom decided it wants to be louder than a tornado siren, announcing a bunch of unnecessary nonsense! On top of all that, she's asking all these personal questions that have nothing to do with this little one isolated incident. As far as I know, it was PROBABLY just a bad batch of Jack!

"Does this really have anything to do with what happened? Because I don't see how this connects." I say, fiddling my fingers, agitated and tired.

"Well, you don't AWS from ONE bottle. This would only result after years of overdrinking finally catching up to you."

She's right... But I knew that already. Starting to feel a bit more shame, I continue to share more.

"It started getting regular after my first semester. By the time senior year hit, before I went to law school, it had become every day..."

"What made you resort to drinking every day?" she asked.

"Well, drinking made me feel like how it looks when you shake a glitter bottle with water, and the glitter finally settles and sinks back to the bottom. It felt like that. I liked that feeling."

I remember the first time it felt like that. I was in my dorm room stressing over finals. I couldn't figure out how to format my essay, and I kept remembering what *he* told me. That I would never be anything and that I was garbage. I needed his voice to go away. So, I went to a nearby store and grabbed my first solo Jack Daniels bottle. I brought it home with me and poured and poured and poured.

Once the voices disappeared, my mind was clear enough for me to write my first paragraph.
Then, they came back, Louder. So, I drank again.
The rest is history. Mostly because I can't remember crap from my last year of college. It was all just one big blur of brown gold liquid filling my brain and covering my ears from the ugliness of the world.

"So, using your symbolism of glitter, what was your glitter? What did you need the liquor to settle?" she asked, placing the clipboard away from her and looking me in the eyes to listen.

"The voices... I didn't want to hear the voices...." My voice starts creaking a little as a warning that I was getting close to opening up beyond my comfort zone.

"When you say voices, what do you mean? What voices were bothering you, Aniyah?"

Too much, this is too much. I can't go into that. I can't do it. I need to tell her, but I can't, not yet. I just shrug and stop looking at her.

"Aniyah, I know it can be scary, but you really need to open up to me so that I can better help you navigate these feelings, and help you try and curb this need for alcohol." She says this not in an angry or frustrating way, but seriously and direct.

I release a BIG exhale before I say...
"*His* voice... I was trying to quiet *his* voice..."

My voice wasn't creaking anymore… but seemingly falling apart into little pieces… like little squeaks of sound…

"You said 'his voice'. Who is 'he'? Did 'he' hurt you in some way?" she asked concerningly, as she picks her clipboard back up.

She started writing, but she didn't keep it with her. Once she finished, she placed it back down and looked at me again. Listening to me intently. Consistent… She's consentient…. I like that.

"*He*… was my mom's boyfriend. *He…*"
I take another pause as I catch myself getting emotional. Tears start to take over my eyes, and I use all my strength to hold them back. Trying to focus on the beating of my heart and on the beeping machine to keep me from breaking down.

With a slight smile of reassurance, the doctor says, "It's okay, Aniyah. You can tell me what happened. I'm here to support you though this…".

Unable to control the overflow of tears in my eyes,

I say with the tiniest of voice, "*He* hurt me... *He* took... EVERYTHING from me..."

At this point, I have no choice but to just let them flow freely. I have no choice but to let... myself... break... And everything comes out... All the tears I've kept inside for 10 years are rushing out of me. All the tears that have been filling my lungs and suffocating me. Gone, just from letting go. I tell her everything, from *him*.... to *Espwa*... to my mom... I held Nothing back. And it felt SO GOOD....

I cried, and I cried, and I cried some more. Every time a big cry came, she would give me some tissue and just sit there listening.

"I should have looked for help before it got this bad." I said weepingly. "I could never do anything right... I couldn't even stop *him*!" I said, invisibly beating myself up for being so weak.

"Aniyah, this was NOT your fault. You were a child. It's not a child's responsibility to protect themselves. You Have to forgive your younger self for what happened to you. That's the Only way you can heal beyond this..." she said with intense compassion. As if she understood.

"How can I forgive myself when I'm still suffering from not saying anything? For not following the rules!"

"No, Aniyah, you're suffering from Shame and Guilt. You are feeling guilty for something someone did to You. You just said earlier that '*HE*' hurt you. You didn't hurt you. And what rules did you break?"

"The girl rules. Like, no tight clothes, no red lipstick, no straight hair... You didn't have those rules?" I asked.

"No matter what you wear, no matter what your hair looks like, if a predator attacks you, it's because there is something wrong with THEM. There is absolutely Nothing wrong with you, your body or your hair. You were a child, and he was a grown man who should have self-control and who shouldn't be attracted to kids. You were a kid,

Aniyah. Nothing was your fault, and you need to realize that."

I was a kid... I WAS a kid. And I shouldn't have had to worry about some pervert being attracted to me. Instead, my mom should have been the one protecting me! She was supposed to protect me from the monsters under the bed, but she became one instead. She was so busy trying to keep her man for whatever reason that she was willing to turn a blind eye to what happened.

If *Espwa* had come to me and told me someone touched her, I would have handled it right then and there because I loved her above all. But that was the problem. My mom loved him more than she would ever even try to love me.

"You know what? You're right. I Didn't deserve what happened to me. And I don't deserve to feel guilty. I Deserve to move on. I Deserve to be happy. I Deserve to LIVE..."

"Aniyah, I am SO Proud of you. You have come a long way even in this conversation! And opening up to share with me you experience shows just how Brave and Strong you are. *Espwa* would have been so proud to have you as her mommy."

Espwa IS proud of me. Even though I've messed up and wasted 10 years of my life, she's still proud of me... In that moment, I began to reflect on my tears. But for the first time in 10 years, I didn't feel embarrassed about them. I'm proud of my tears. They are a war cry to every thought that has tried to destroy me. Every word that has tried to crush me. My tears tell them that I'm not gone yet.

"So, does this mean I have to go to rehab?"
I asked with my voice destroyed from crying.

"Well, you can definitely benefit from some counseling and support though this journey. So I think you should still try outpatient rehab. Oh! And I have something else very special for you. Hold on really quick while I grab it from my office. I'll be right back!" she says as she leaves excitedly.

She comes back with a small clear Mason jar, all different colors of glitter, a few small bottles of water and glue. I wonder what it's for. Maybe it's just an arts and crafts she does with all her patients.

"I want you to create something called a stress jar. This jar is supposed to symbolize your stress and voices that try to cause you to drink. When you shake the jar, you are taking control of your feelings and watching them ease, as you watch the glitter fall and stop moving. So, when you get the urge to drink as a means to calm down, use this instead!" says as she places the box on my lap. She gives me the directions, and I go crazy on the glitter. I use black, purple, blue, pink, and brown! I use brown to symbolize my mind giving me the urge to drink.

"So, before I go, I want to say again that I am proud of you, Aniyah. I'm glad you have made the brave decision to open up to me and complete the first step towards healing; admitting that you need it." She smiles as she gets ready to leave.

"Thank you for helping me with everything. I never thought I could feel this at ease without being filled with liquor." I say with a slight chuckle. She says you're welcome and leaves, closing the door behind her. I shake my glitter jar and watch it settle. I repeat this about 10 times before my eyes fall with the glitter, and I fall asleep. I'm Finally Resting...

****

I can't wait till I get the courage to go.
I can't wait till I finally say no...
When I leave just know imma be ok.
When I leave just know imma be ok.
When I leave just know imma be ok.
When I leave just know...

When I Leave
- *Asia Pearson*

****

Chapter 23:

March 30th, 2023
THE FINAL CHAPTER

I've never felt so Free... I've never felt this
open, new, and fresh. I have been seeing my old
therapist consistently for over a month now, and she
has helped me tremendously. I haven't had any
alcohol since the incident. I've been sobered for a
whole month and 2 weeks. I am still in shock!
I can't believe I'm doing it! I'm not exactly happy,
but I'm getting there, and I am beyond ok with that.

If I were to tell my 15-year-old self that I am in this
peaceful place right now, she would think I was
lying. But I did it. I opened my mouth, and I got
HELP. I no longer have to hold the burden of what
happened to me on my own anymore.
Every day, I CHOOSE Myself.
Every day, I fight to keep this feeling.

And every day, GOD shows me more and more
PEACE.

I prayed for the first time 2 weeks ago when I saw a
celebrity post on Instagram that they were starting a
consistent journey of healing her confidence and
building a relationship with GOD. She inspired me
so much that I decided to join the group she created!
And we have all been helping each other stay on
track with GOD ever since.

I miss *Espwa* EVERY Moment of EVERY Day…

I often think about how life would be if she were
here. But it's different now. Those scenarios used to
make me sad, and I used to try to drink to get them
out of my head. But now, I invite them in. It's like
my way of letting *Espwa* know all the way in
heaven that her momma cares about her and "loves
her like a bird". My grandma always told me that. I
still don't know exactly what that means, but I know
it's special, and that is what *Espwa* will always be to
me, special.

I finally have a community around me. Tuchelianna and I go on girls' days once a week to different places around the city. I'm having so much fun with that. True and Good FUN.

I ordered some skincare items from Amazon. They will be here in 4 days, so I will start a morning and nighttime routine. I am so grateful. Peace is not temporary, it's something you always have access to. You just have to take the time to **LOOK IN THE MIRROR** and start healing from the things in your past that are holding you back from grabbing PEACE.

I have also been going to my AA meetings. At first, I felt out of place, but then the people there started introducing themselves to me, and we all started to share stories. Now I really like going. It's full of people who struggle just like me. It's full of people who are fighting for their control and their autonomy, just like me. It's really kind of incredible to see these people's journeys along with mine. It makes me feel less alone. Some people even gave me some suggestions on how to fight urges and cravings.

Speaking of cravings, I really want a donut. So I grab my keys and head to a coffee shop near my house that I didn't even know existed. No more Jack or Brandy. My fix is coffee now. And even though coffee is almost as expensive as my old fix, it's a lot cheaper than losing my life.

I'm standing in line, and this guy who is finer than Trevor Jackson (*and it's Extremely hard to be finer than Trevor, by the way*) is looking down at his phone and bumps into me by accident. He spills the coffee he just picked up all over my clothes.

"Oh no! I'm so sorry! This was all my fault; I wasn't paying attention…" he says while grabbing napkins from the nearest table. I freeze in fear, but for the first time ever, it wasn't because he is a man and talking to me. It was actually because he is literally the most handsome man in the world, and I have no idea what to say back! Then I remembered the last time I had something spilled on me, and I laugh and smile at the difference in my life in such a short amount of time.

"Oh it's fine. I wasn't going anywhere special. My name is Aniyah, by the way." I say, wiping off my shirt with the napkins he gave me.

"My name is Isiah. Please, let me pay for your coffee. That's the least I can do to pay you back for using your clothes for target practice." We laugh, forgetting for a moment that I'm in line and that there are 5 people behind me.

"It's fine. I got it. Thank you, though. I appreciate the gesture." I smile and blush a little as I begin to give my order to the barista.

Isiah interjects again, "Well, if I can't buy your coffee, can I take you out to dinner one day this week? My treat of course." he says while giving me a convincing smirk. I'm definitely still scared to go on dates, but I promised myself that I am no longer allowing fear to rule my life! And I am sticking to that.

"Ok, let's try for Friday!" I sigh deeply because I can't believe I just got a date. My first date in my entire life!

Wow... it's REALLY happening for Me...

Finally...

TO BE CONTINUED......

Their Story...

Now that you have heard Aniyah's story, I am going to introduce to you two real survivors and allow them the opportunity to share their stories and how they have overcome them.

When you read their stories, I want you to connect with them and their experience. And if you are a survivor, I want you to see yourself in them, and know that if they can survive, so can you.

THANK YOU, Martasia and Asia for trusting me with your stories and allowing me to share them with the world.

This is my final message to you in this book:

No Mirror is Unfixable.
No Towel is Too Dirty.
And if You are Still Breathing,
You... CAN... Heal...

Asia's Story...

Age when it started: 4 years old

Where were you?: At a family member's house

Age when it ended?: 8 or 9 years old

Witnesses?: No one saw

What happened:

In my experience, molestation became an adult video and self-pleasuring addiction at a very young age. Unknowingly through my unawareness of shame, I grew depressed and contemplated "un-aliving" (*self-harming*) myself until I was 17.

Interestingly though, I was very prideful about losing my virginity, so I didn't lose my virginity until I felt it was appropriate and with someone I felt I could genuinely trust. (*I was 19 when I lost my virginity*). However, after losing my virginity & entering a relationship where I fell in love, the character traits I had unknowingly developed from the trauma of many childhood experiences, including molestation, started to show up in the relationship. I was accustomed to not speaking up for myself. Not knowing when to fight for myself or for others; I'd shut down and suppress my feelings instead of communicating. I realized that I was a people pleaser (*putting others' needs in front of mine*), and I realized that I lacked the concept of having boundaries. It took me many mistakes and unfortunate events throughout that relationship of almost 10 years to leave and face the molestation head-on (***Looking In the Mirror...***).

I broke up with my boyfriend out of anger and shortly after tried to mend the relationship. I was denied and told to go and find out why I always run away when things get hard, so I did a week later. Out of 5 offenses, I spoke to the 4 family members I had those encounters with and talked about the molestation. It went much better than I had ever imagined throughout the years. Some remembered some did not, but all were very apologetic.

That weight lifted a world of insecurity off of me. I was finally able to see myself for the beauty I always had. GOD began to heal me daily, revealing the many issues and ways I had adopted because I suppressed my pain for a long time. And I can proudly say that I no longer walk with that very dark cloud of shame and pain.

I AM FREE! With GOD, I Survived it ALL!
I AM ASIA PEARSON, AND THIS IS MY STORY!

****

THERAPY
BY ASIA PEARSON
(a song I wrote about my experience)

Maybe I need therapy

Cause I won't talk, I'd rather shut down

Maybe I need therapy

When you talk to me I get offended somehow

Cause after you hurt my feelings

I don't want no kind of dealings

Everything you said

I'm feeling triggered in so many ways

I've been through so much

All my life I felt alone

Been struggling with trust

I just want to feel like you want me

Insecurities form from mental instabilities

I shouldn't put that all on you

Even though that you really hurt me too

Let's talk about my abandonment issues

Let's talk about how I was touched and abused

Why would I think I could ever

love you through this pain?

You didn't do that to me

I guess I need therapy…

****

Martasia's Story...

Age when it started: 6 or 7 years old

Where were you?: At the predator's home. I was only supposed to be there for the summer, but ended up staying with them for a long time.

Age when it ended: 8 or 9 years old

Witnesses?: He would wait till everyone was sleep so no one was up.

What happened:

My sister struggled with homosexuality, and she married a guy because she couldn't come out to our family due to fear of rejection. I guess because she wasn't giving him the sexual attention he felt he deserved due to her women, he assumed he could just get it from me.

He would wait till she and the rest of the family were asleep. He would pull down my pajamas and touch me. If I tried to wake up or get up and move, he would put my head down, and I didn't fully understand what was happening. I realized it was wrong when my brother caught him doing it to me. My brother was older than me; however, I felt like the big sister.

When he caught the molester assaulting me, he was going to tell my family, but the molester threatened him with a gun. The gun scared him more than it scared me. After that, I "allowed" it to happen because, I didn't want him to hurt my young niece living in the household.

I never felt resentment towards my niece due to it though, because I thought that by the time she was my age, I could defend her or teach her how to defend herself. However, my niece was sick and ended up dying young. Even after her death, it continued; until I left to live with my father after my sister got sick. I told my dad about what happened in 2004. My sister passed away in 2009 from her sickness. Even though I told my father what had happened, he still allowed the molester to be at the funeral. I didn't tell my father when it happened because I didn't think he would do anything.

My father wasn't emotionally present. He provided, that's all. We had to figure out everything else ourselves. Even though she didn't know what happened, I blamed my mother. I hated her for a long time, because if she hadn't left us with our dad and picked us up when she was supposed to, we would never have had to live with my sister, and this would have never happened.

Since I had very few examples of healthy relationships, I became very promiscuous and angry with men when I got older. Even though I didn't have sex till I was 17years old, I felt like sex wasn't a big thing. I felt I should just give men what they want, which is sex, because they will take it anyway.

I started fighting constantly and being very angry with everyone around me. When I eventually got into many toxic and abusive relationships, I didn't think that the sexual abuse had anything to do with it. I felt more like it was only because of the emotional absence of my father. It felt like the only men I would attract would be emotionally unavailable. I never got to tell my father how I felt and how much his emotional absence impacted my life, because he passed away when I was 17 years old. However, I did get a chance to tell my mother.

When I talked to my mother, I realized that my mother was just as human as me and didn't really understand or know how to be a good mother. My mother took accountability, which I appreciated. She not only took responsibility, but she also tries to be an active grandparent to my children.

I also talked with my brother, and even though I didn't blame him for staying quiet, he apologized for not protecting me. It's been hard living life with children and trauma. I have a partner now who has not proven to be a danger to my kids; however, I still get scared whenever I leave them together in a room.

I'm always on guard, but hopefully, one day, as I continue to have an open dialogue with my kids and my partner, my anxiety will ease…

MY NAME IS MARTASIA RICHARDSON, AND THIS IS MY STORY!

About the Book

*"**Looking in the Mirror**" ignites a whirlwind of emotions and experiences that end on a hopeful note. Jayla takes the readers on a journey of negativing traumatic experiences while opening the door to start the conversation around often overlooked topics.*

Through relatable language, she exposes the fight against stigmas and shares the stories of brave women who pulled themselves together with little support and are now SURVIVORS!

Great job! Incredibly proud of your courage, boldness, and passion surrounding this topic!

*- **Ember S. Lomax***

This book is beyond phenomenal. It takes the reader to a place that is familiar to some and an introduction to others. The book will certainly bring reflection and tears, but most importantly this book brings healing. GOD can heal a broken heart he just needs the pieces, the strength of this book will definitely help those that have been traumatized by their past to collect the pieces and place them at the feet of the Master.

*- **Deon Hayes***

Acknowledgements

First, I would like to thank GOD, the head of my life. For
giving me this message that is so very urgent!
I could thank many people for their part in writing this book,
but I would run out of paper and time in this world.
So, if you do not see your name in these acknowledgments and
you were a part of this process, THANK YOU!!!

****

To my mother, Lakita Howery...
I want to thank my mom for allowing me to write this book
and chase my dreams. I Love You, Mom. She's the Real OG!

To my inspiration, Trarina Paige...
This fantastic playwriter, director, producer, and author
inspired me with her play, *"The Rise of a Fallen Tamar"*,
which tells the story of the biblical character Tamar, who was
sexually assaulted by her half-brother Amnon. After
confessing this assault to her father, he did not believe her and
punished her while protecting the predator.

The play gave me the motivation and reassurance that
"Looking In the Mirror" was an important story that needed
to be told. It showed me the power and effect creativity can
have on a community. So, thank you, TeeTee!

To my teacher, Mrs. Kucera...
This was my 8th grade Social Studies teacher and the first
person I ever let read the draft of chapter one. She helped me
to believe that my activism was important. She encouraged me
to be bold and to never let anyone take my voice. She also
helped me learn from different perspectives and opinions.
So, thank you, Mrs. Kucera! You will always have a place in
my heart.

To my grandmother, Jaye Anderson...
My grandmother is my best friend and my go-to person. She has always been there for me for anything and everything, especially this book. She inspired me to keep going even when I didn't want to, and I felt it wasn't good enough. Sometimes she was more excited about this book than I was! I Love You, Granny! Thank you.

To my favorite library assistant, Ms. Berry...
Every time I wrote a new chapter, she would read it, help me with anything I needed, kept me encouraged and always pushed me to do More. And if someone tried to convince me to stop writing or called it "too dark", she would defend me right then and there and call anybody out in order to protect the vision GOD gave me. So, thank you, Ms. Berry!

To my auntie, Robyn...
I have known her since I was 8, and ever since I've known her, she has always been willing to go to war for me. Just for that, I am grateful. When I told her my idea about this book, she was down for it 10000%. She has also been a creative help on this project! So, thank you, Auntie Robyn!

****

About the Author

Jayla Anderson Westbrook grew up in Chicago, IL. She grew up in the Apostolic church, where she loved music and singing. She has six siblings, five living and one deceased.

Jayla loved writing from an early age. She always got a 100% on creative writing assignments since 3rd grade. Even though writing is one of her biggest passions, Jayla aspires to become a lawyer so that she can continue to use her voice like she uses her writing in her books to fight for justice.

Jayla has started not-for-profit organizations; for example, during her 8th-grade year, she started the *'Can You Hear Us'* organization, where she and a group of students and teachers took issues that challenged their ability to succeed in school and brought them to the school board to get these issues resolved.

Jayla has always and will always fight for the prospering and justice of the black community, even if that means being criticized or bullied.

She will NOT be silenced...

Contributors
and References

Music Rights:
2Pac/ Shakur, Tupac- "Brenda's Got a Baby"
2Pacalypse Now, Interscope Records, (1991).

Tweet/ Keys Charlene- "Drunk",
Southern Hummingbird, Warner Music Group, (2002).

Franklin, Kirk- "Help Me Believe", The Fight of My Life,
Sony BMG Music Entertainment, (2007).

Ellish, Billie/Robinson, Khalid- "Lovely", 13 Reasons Why
Season 2, Darkroom and Interscope Records, (2018).

Tweet/ Keys Charlene- "I Was Created For This",
Charlene, Entertainment One, (2016).

Trainor Megan - "Superwoman", Taken' It Back,
Epic Records, (2022).

Solange Knowles- "Cranes In the Sky", A Seat at the Table,
Saint Records and Columbia Records, (2016).

Lennon John- "Beautiful Boy (Darling Boy)",
Double Fantasy, Geffen Records, (1980).

Empire Cast, Bozeman, Veronica- "What is Love",
Empire Original Soundtrack From Season 1,
Columbia Records, (2015).

Goo Goo Dolls- "Iris", Dizzy Up the Girl,
Warner Bros. Records, (1998).

Pearson Asia- "Therapy" and "When I Leave",
Therapy, All Wins Entertainment, (2022).

Contributing Authors:

Ember S. Lomax,
Made for More (2020), *Destined to Thrive: Be Inspired.
Be Empowered* (2020), *Thrive Journal* (2021).
Thrive with Ember

Trarina Paige,
They're All Going to Laugh at You (2021).
**Purpose to Laugh Productions, LLC
Trarina Washington Productions**

Deon Hayes,
Having an Affair with Faith (2016).